Bloom

Bloom:
Progress Not Perfection

Jessica Petty

Editors: Morgan Haller & Kaitlin Marold

Illustrations: Lauren Waselik

Jessica Petty
2019

First Printing: 2019

ISBN <978-0-359-68107-5>

Jessica Petty
Hackettstown, New Jersey 07840

PlaceOfperfectiOn.tumblr.com

This book is a compilation of writings that span over years of my life, over relationships, heartbreaks, self-hatred, learning, and the path towards gaining some form of self-love. They are anything but perfect, but they are raw, real, experiences that I wouldn't change for the world.

If you find yourself in the words on these pages know in your heart you have changed my life in one way or another. You have contributed to the person I am today, whether it be through love, heartbreak, or helping me on my never-ending path towards self-love. *A special thanks goes out to you, you now own a physical piece of my heart and mind, forever.*

To the ones that broke my heart

I kissed you like no one else,
your lips were like the air,
and I couldn't breathe without them
pressed tightly against mine.
But now your lips,
absent from mine
have me here gasping for breath.

I spent so much of my time and effort loving everyone else, that somewhere along the way I'd forgotten how to love myself.

I'm always a maybe,
or a sometimes.
Just once I'd like to be an everything
or an always.

I am not one to hold hands
but if you asked,
I'd make an exception.
I am not one to cry,
but if you dared to say goodbye,
I would shed a river.
I am not one to fall for someone,
but baby when you smiled.
I am not one to give up,
but when you whispered "sorry",
I knew in that moment none of it mattered.
Because you were saying goodbye,
while I was saying see you later.

My parents never warned me about pain,
not the pain of falling off your bike
or scraping your knee.
More importantly,
no one ever warned me about the pain of a heartbreak,
to not believe in fairytales or prince charmings.
Pain, it comes in many different forms
but I've come to realize that you can't have pain
without love,
and in that moment I realized,
whether I wanted to believe it or not, I was in love with
you.
I know that some people are meant to fall for each
other,
but not meant to be together.
So, I guess I'll just walk away,
and hope that one day we'll be following the same
path again.

Parts of you have become parts of me. I hope you always lift your feet when you go over railroad tracks. And I hope you always touch the roof when you rush through a yellow light. I hope you knock on your head three times and kiss your knuckles with the same excitement I kissed your cheek. I hope sunflowers always remind you to stand tall and strong. I hope when you drive you sing at the top of your lungs even if no one's there to listen. Your laugh is contagious. I hope you laugh, not that fake laugh you did sometimes, but the one that starts in your belly and explodes from your soul. I hope you reach into your pockets, backpack, and glove box and find chapstick strategically placed everywhere. I hope you flip the coin, take a drive, and maybe one day it will lead you back to me.

I wish that I could choose who I would fall in love with, because then maybe I could finally choose to start loving myself.

I remember our first kiss as if it were yesterday,
no memory more vivid.
Yet we were so intoxicated,
not just the drugs or the alcohol.
I was intoxicated on the thought of you,
on the way your hands felt on my body.
The moment your hands touched me,
I knew it was inevitable.
The way you looked into my eyes,
it made me feel alive for the first time.
I'll never forget the way that my heart raced,
the butterflies fluttering in my stomach,
or the anticipation in the air.
They say that some people are meant to have a last kiss,
but I think that we were only meant for a *first.*

When I stare into your eyes
and you stare back into mine,
I see emptiness where love used to lie.
I don't see just the surface,
I see the lies in which they hide.
And who knows,
if I'll ever look into your eyes
and see the view they used to provide.
And for those few moments,
I wonder,
what do you think
while you're searching in my eyes,
because it isn't "I love you."

I'm not sure why things happened the way they did, I'm not sure why we met on the first of May, and I'm not sure why I ended up in M.O. Sometimes I still think about it all. But I do not regret it, that year taught me more about life, love, and most importantly myself than I ever thought possible. I became a better version of myself because of it. You taught me what I want in someone; and what I should expect from someone, I hope my future wife has some of the qualities I loved about you. You taught me to look for someone who will cover my room in sticky notes, or buy a huge bear just because I'm sad. You taught me to look for someone who will hold me as I sob uncontrollably on the bathroom floor, and not look at me any differently because of it. In a way because of you, I learned what it was like to love someone with a mental illness. I watched you love me through it, and in a way it taught me how to love myself through it. I didn't know it at the time, but I do now. Some days I was so sad I didn't even have the energy to wash my own hair, and so you did it for me. I would shake and so you would hold me every night. When I thought I couldn't ever smile again you sang to me in the car. I am not sure why things ever happened the way that they did, but a tiny piece of me is happy that they did. I have washed my hair without the help of your fingertips 74 times, I have slept tangled in blankets rather than in your arms for 63 nights, I have driven countless miles with an empty passenger seat, I have listened to hundreds of songs without your voice belting the lyrics. I never wanted things to end the way they did. I'm not sure why things happened the way they did, but I am thankful that they did. Hurting me is the best thing you ever did for me, because of you I have learned to love myself. You hurting me forced me to learn to love myself without the help from you. And I am a stronger me than we ever were an us.

It has been 365 days since I kissed you last, but if that's true why can I still taste you on my lips.

"I'm gonna be so lucky to have you one day."
Well when one day rolls around,
someone else will be lucky.
Someone else will be holding my hand,
kissing me in a way I thought only you could.
They will be lucky enough to have my heart,
and hopefully they won't shatter it
into a million pieces the way you did.
So fuck your one day,
because your luck just ran out.

They say everything happens for a reason,
that good things fall apart so better things can fall together,
and time heals all wounds.
But I don't understand this reason.
Not only did great things fall apart,
but so did I.
It's been months and I still don't feel whole.
My heart,
it aches when I see you.
How can we pass each other and pretend we were nothing?
Like we didn't spend countless nights wrapped in each other.
Like I don't know the feeling of your body on mine.
I remember being so excited to see you,
I would run and jump into your arms.
Now,
we walk silently passed one another.
No running, no jumping, no laughs, or hugs
and I wonder,
What happened?
What changed?
And then I realized your heart no longer races to me,
and so I jumped
but there was no one there to catch me.

It's pouring here at home.
I stood outside in the rain,
just as we had done so many times before.
I stared up into the starry sky,
and I just sat and cried.
Tears streaming down my face,
racing against the tears shed by the sky.
As I cried harder,
the world, it thundered and boomed
sounding just as broken as I was.
They say that home is where the heart is,
well baby its pouring here at home.

It's been months
but I still think of you every day.
I want to erase you
I want to forget what you look like
when I roll over in the morning.
I want to forget your smile
or the way your skin smelled.
I want to forget how you made me feel alive
for the first time.
What a strange thing it is to be breathing
but to no longer feel alive.
I want to erase you from my memory
yet I can't do that without erasing parts of me.

I remember how you would hold my hand
tracing every line and imperfection
as if I was the most beautiful piece of art.
I remember how you would look at me
as if I were the only girl in the room,
like no one else existed to you.
Now your eyes meet mine,
sad, cold, and angry.
It's been months since I've felt your touch,
I never understood what changed.
But then I saw you look at her.
The look in your eyes, it wasn't gone,
only no longer reserved for me.
I guess I'll always have to wonder
why it is you decided to leave
and eventually she'll wonder,
she'll wonder just like me.

She looks to the stars,
the moon,
the galaxies,
and everything in between.
Searching for something
to fill the void
caused by what she used to find
looking at you.

If I had to describe the way we used to be,
I would say that we were like the ocean and the shore.
Touching every once in a while,
but when the two separate,
the beach feels empty.
The same way my heart does now that the tide is out.

You told me that you loved my freckles,
now I spend hours trying to cover them.
The same way I'm left trying to mend
the cracks in my heart.

They told me love was one of the best feelings I'd ever discover.
They told me it would make me see the world in a different light.
Told me it would make me feel alive.
They told me that love was something that everyone should experience.
But what they didn't tell me,
they didn't tell me that when it's over,
it feels like someone ripped your heart out of your chest to keep for their own personal gain.
They didn't tell me that I would feel so hollow,
as if someone reached inside of me and took out everything that I am.
They didn't tell me I would spend my nights lying awake, crying myself to sleep in agony.
They didn't tell me that sometimes when you fall in love with someone they don't always love you back.
They told me that love is something everyone should experience,
but I wouldn't wish this on anyone.

Goodbye
We said our goodbyes,
but the thing is we've said them
a thousand times before.
But somehow
we always end up back at hello,
I miss you,
I need you.
Soon enough our hellos turned into
"I need some time to think"
But I guess that you're done thinking,
because now you've left it at goodbye,
when I've been waiting for hello.

You told me not to worry,
told me it was just a kiss.
Told me it was before our time,
you told me not to worry,
so I tried not to.
But then I saw the way you looked at her,
you thought it went unnoticed.
I saw the way you hugged for just a little too long
but still, I tried not to worry.
I said to myself “she’s mine so it’s okay”.
Then you said it was just one kiss,
and it won’t happen again.
So again, I tried not to worry,
but then you told me you didn't love me anymore
and I knew it was because of her.
You stopped looking at me
and you started looking to her.
And dear god, I hope she worries.

Do not judge a book by its cover, but that's what you did with me isn't it? You saw something you wanted, so you picked it up, read the pages, learned the story. It's supposed to be the reader falling in love with the writer, with the story. You're supposed to read it over and over. Until the pages are so creased you can barely read the words, when you've got paper cuts from constantly flipping pages, and there's coffee stains from your favorite mug. But instead when you were done with me you put me on a shelf. When all I wanted to do was read you over and over again, because for me you were my favorite story. But for you *I was just another book on the shelf.*

I'm afraid that I'll flinch one too many times when you go to touch me out of habit, so maybe one day you'll stop trying to touch me at all.

I'm afraid of sleeping with you because I will learn how my body fits with yours, how your breathing slows in your sleep, and how it feels to wake up and kiss you good morning. And I'm afraid then I'll roll over one morning, but you won't be there anymore.

And I guess I thought if I painted the ocean enough times I'd be able to drown the thoughts of you. But here we are countless canvases later, and I'm still the only thing that's drowning.

Blasting music in my ears trying to drown out the thoughts of you, but I'll lose my hearing before the thought of you ever leaves my mind.

You once asked me why I never wrote about you, and I told you my writing stems from pain and heartbreak, and so you said, “then I hope you never have anything to write about ever again.” I’m driving around and the thoughts, the lines are just running through my head all over again. But I’m afraid to put them down on paper because that means I’m writing again, and we all know what that means.

You know how when you go to the doctor complaining that something hurts, they ask you “is it a sharp pain?”, “a dull pain?”, “does it come and go or is it always there?” The missing you, it hurts. It’s like a dull pain in my heart that never goes away. It never leaves. And if it does it’s for a split second and then it’s a sharp pain. A pain that makes me remember every kiss, every hug, every coffee date, or morning spent burning pancakes. The pain of missing you never leaves. There is no medication. No magic fix. The dull pain in my chest never leaves. It’s like the weight of the world is sitting on my chest. In the same place you used to lay your head ever so lightly. The only cure for this is *you*.

I should stop drinking, but there are so many things I should stop. Yes drinking; drinking is one of them, but more than that one of them is you. I should stop liking. Stop calling. Stop thinking. So many things I should stop doing, thinking about you is the biggest one. But here I am. Still drinking and still thinking about you.

"If we can't grow together, we must grow apart." This was the reasoning I gave myself for so long without really understanding the meaning of the words. I never thought I would grow apart from you. You were tangled in every piece of me. The roots ran so deep that by trying to cut them out you took pieces of me with you. They left holes behind, but in place of those holes grew flowers, grew trees, grew plants I had never seen before. Without those roots tangled in me I was so free to grow, and everything around me became brighter after a while. New parts of me grew and grew and grew until I was unrecognizable. I never thought that growing apart from you would only be the beginning of my growth.

You know what hurts my heart?
That someone can be so much to you, everything really, for so long, and in a matter of moments, seconds really, that person becomes nothing. All of the good becomes tainted by the bad, the anger, the fights, all the words you never thought you'd say, and all of a sudden you can't remember what that everything really felt like. Even though at the time it made you feel so much happiness, love, and compassion. You take down the pictures, rip up the love letters, you remove them from your sight, hide it all, put it in a box and throw it under your bed. Only to be pulled out when your mind is racing and your heart is heavy. Yet somewhere deep down they're still sitting there, still hiding in the bottom of your heart. Taking up one tiny little piece for the rest of your life, where the memories, the laughs, and the kisses all hide. You were everything to me for so long and now you're just a box under my bed.

October 17, 2017
Someone else washed my hair today.

I just wanna go home, but home is a faraway place in a heart where the love for me no longer exists.

My fingers do not dance around my head as yours did while washing away the harshness of the day.

I want to hate you, I want to hate everything about you. I want to hate your laugh, your smile, or the color of your eyes. All of the things I ever loved about you, I want to hate them. I want to hate you. All those things I loved about you, the way you drive too fast, or sing too loud in the car, the way you laugh till you cry with a little scream mixed in, I want to hate them because I know she's loving them now. She's loving all the parts of you I loved. I wonder if there's any of my love left on them. I wonder if sometimes you're driving and you look into your passenger seat only to remember what I looked like sitting there smiling up at you or sleeping on your center console. I wonder if you'll find my chapstick in your glove box and maybe you'll put it on, just because it's there. But will you wish my lips were applying it to yours as they always had? I want to *HATE* everything about you, but I cannot because I cannot stop *LOVING YOU.*

I have been drunk every day for nearly two weeks now. I don't know if I'm trying to numb some kind of pain, or if I'm trying to actually get myself to feel something. But shot after shot, drink after drink, I'm left just as empty as the glass.

The Sun and Her Flowers

You bought me this book for valentine's day last year. Every love poem inside it made my heart beat with purpose. For you, for us, for the future I saw inside my mind with every passing word. I read this book and saw you in the pages. Here I am nearly a year later picking the book up again, but here I sit reading the same poems that set my heart on fire. Yet all they ignite now is long lost memories. "I love you's" left unsaid. The future lost inside the fights. With each passing poem those words lose their meaning, the same way the girl that gave me this book has.
You lit the fire inside my soul then put it out all on your own.

Your apologies came in colorful bouquets, but never in words.

The Letters Left Unsent

To the little boy in the back seat,

I'm writing this to you because I know one day, when you're old enough to understand it, I will give it to you. And maybe it will help you to understand me. Me, your momma, is only 20 years old when writing this. It's odd to even say that, me someone's momma? It seems unimaginable, yet so within reach at the same time. I want to tell you this, you do not exist yet, nor does the remote possibility of you, but you are everything. At 19 years old I was at rock bottom. I was self-destructive, sad, small, and suicidal to say the least. I wanna tell you about someone. Her name is Hannah. Maybe she's your momma today, and maybe I've never mentioned her before. But when my eyes drift off for a little too long, or I seem galaxies away that's where I am. I'm with her, baby. You see, you were ours, and then you were just mine. Let me tell you how you came about. Hannah woke me up one morning, to tell me about her dream. She said that we were on a road trip just as the two of us always were, and always would be, and I was of course asleep in the passenger seat; you know what car rides do to me. She woke me up and asked me if I wanted to stop for food, which is when I turned around to the backseat of the car and said "sweetie are you hungry", only for Hannah to then look back and see, well you. This small little boy with curly brown hair and the brightest blue eyes, staring back up at us. The perfect mixture of the two of us. You. You are what kept me going, what keeps me going. I remember when the fighting would get really bad, when one of us thought the other might leave, or not love each other anymore you would hear "I call little boy in the back seat" and it would all stop. The racing in my brain, the anger, the fear, everything. Because of you. I can remember sitting on the top of a parking garage ready to jump, on my bathroom floor at 2 a.m. with a blade in my hand, or with an open bottle of sleeping pills sitting on my nightstand. And she would say, please think about the little boy in the backseat, I need you to be his momma. On every bad day I thought of you. Of us. Of our life together. You kept me going. And even after your momma left, especially after your momma left. You are what kept me going. I've stayed alive for you. I've stayed alive for the little boy in the backseat who isn't so little anymore.

To my first love,

8/12/14 “I left for college today, I thought of you. And how we had always talked about how we would hug for hours and never want to let go. Now I’m wondering if you’re holding her in your arms at this very moment.”

8/26/14 “It’s hard here, I wish I had you to talk to.”

9/13/14 “It’s my birthday today. I wish I was spending it with you like last year..”

10/02/14 “I thought I was done with this, with you. But its 2 am and I’m wide awake, tears streaming down my face. Still wondering, why?

10/10/14 “God I fucking miss you, why don’t you care”

10/11/14 “I don’t know why I’m thinking about you so much lately , I think it’s this time of year. I still miss you even though I’ll never say it out loud.”

10/29/14 “It’s almost Halloween, your favorite holiday, yes I remembered. I remember every little detail about you. From the smell of your skin to the way you’d inhale when you held me in your arms. I wonder if she loves that about you too.”

To the kids who suffered in silence, I understand.

Children are known for being afraid of the dark, afraid of the monsters in the closet, and the boogieman under their bed. Mommies and daddies are expected to check to make sure it's safe before they tuck their little ones in. But what if your monsters didn't disappear when the sun rose or the lights came back on? Everyone says that high school will be the best four years of your life, meeting new people, making friends, playing sports, just simply having a carefree time. From the outside it may have looked like I had that experience, but when classes, dances, and practices were over the makeup comes off and the truth comes out. While girls my age spent hours experimenting with new makeups to make them look 5 years older than they actually were, I spent my time trying to figure out which shade of concealer would best cover the various shades of black and blue that sat perched on my cheek. While all of my friends eagerly broke out their new summer clothes, sundresses, tanktops, and shorts they would most likely get in trouble for wearing, I sported a long-sleeved hoodie because tanned skin is cute, but bruised not so much. When dealing with something so heavy. You begin to notice the sadness in the people around you, how their smiles no longer reach their ears, or how the sparkle has left their eye, their laughs are no longer full but forced and fake. You begin to wonder how many of the people around you are surrounded, drowning in the darkness the same way that you are. Although we can see others struggling, losing the light behind their eyes, no one ever says or does anything about it. It's as though they think by touching on the topic, they will somehow be infected by this dark cloud. It's the topic no one ever talks about. It's like the dirty secret we all keep locked away in the closet, but no matter how many locks you put on that door it will seep out of every corner. You'd be surprised just how many social workers, teachers, police men, etc. will give you "the look". The one that says yes, this is sad but there's not much I can do about it. I've come, looked, done my job, so now I'll go home to my bed, in my nice safe house, and I'll forget about the little girl we found hiding in her closet, shaking in fear. They won't hesitate to deem your situation "okay" not for lack of bruises, tears, or cries for help, but because the situation "just isn't severe enough" or "isn't immediate danger". So how about tonight we switch places and you can hide in my closet and you can endure the wrath. And then please tell me the situation isn't immediate, and surely it can't be severe. But that's okay because "out of sight out of mind", *for those not involved that is.*

January 19th, 2017 / In the little white journal.

There are officially 3 different years wrapped up into this book now. It's nearing 1:30 in the morning. I have no idea why I'm sitting here at my desk, writing this to you. But here I am. Exactly where I always end up, back at you. I read this journal tonight, from front to back. I've continued writing in it, even after you left. I don't know, it became a way of saying what I never could out loud. But anyways, I noticed something I began writing in this journal in pen and it stayed that way for a long time until somewhere along the line I began writing in pencil, and all the entries up until this one have remained that way. I think subconsciously I knew. When we began I was so sure, so in love. I was so unbelievably sure that we would make it, and along the way there were some scribbles here and there, until I was scribbling out half a page or ripping it out completely. I became so scared. So insecure. So unsure. Hence the pencil. If I said anything wrong, I could erase it. I could go back, change the story. Right? Go back and erase the bad, leave the good, and rewrite the ending. The ending where we're together. Happily with our three little ones in a tiny home somewhere in the middle of Oklahoma. It could change. Right? Well this, this is pen. There's no erasing, no changing, no rewrites. In this story there's just, well, *the end.*

To her parents,

I think about you all the time; I think about what I would say if I ever saw you again. It's nearly one in the morning months after I've last seen your daughter but the sight of her never leaves my mind, let alone my heart. And so, I would tell you this, you have raised one hell of a child. I have learned from her much of what she learned from you, the values you instilled in her, and the morals you have given her. I would tell you that because of her, because of you, I am who I am today. You saved my life. Your daughter saved my life. I am forever indebted to you and your family. Because of you I have seen love, compassion, empathy, and every quality I desire to have in my life. The countless holidays spent with you and your family in the home that once just felt like a house to me have changed me forever. You created a daughter so strong, so relentless, so caring, so compassionate, and overall such an amazing human being that I am forever in awe of her. I am convinced I will never meet another young woman or family that means as much to me as yours has. I would say thank you, as I said to you that first week you met me on your living room couch, thank you, thank you for opening up your home and your hearts to me as I know it must not have been easy, as I have until now been a stranger to you. Thank you for letting me meet your daughter, as she means more to me than you could ever imagine, I love her more than you will ever know, and I always will. You hugged me after that and then she came down the stairs and it was our secret. I would say those very words to you again, but I would say this, thank you, thank you for letting me meet your daughter as she has saved my life. She has made me into a better person than I ever believed I could have been. Thank you for being my family when I needed one the most. I hope to one day be even half the mother you are to her and were to me. And I hope to raise my daughter to be exactly like yours even if it isn't your granddaughter. Thank you, thank you for letting me meet your daughter.

To the ones I've loved

I used to drive a hundred miles an hour down the highway and feel nothing. No excitement, no fear, nothing. Now I go over 80 and my heart skips a beat and I lean towards the brake.

When my mind wanders
it goes straight to you.
When my heart beats faster
it's because you're on my mind.
When someone touches my arm
I wait for the goosebumps I felt from your touch.
When someone takes a deep breath
I think back to the last breath before we kissed.
The last breath of pure air
before it was flooded with desire,
before I was left gasping for breath.
Yet I didn't care, and I would struggle to breathe all night,
if it meant I could stay wrapped in your arms.

Your touch awakened my body as if I'd been asleep for years.

Drunken Paradise

I think that drunken texts
and intoxicated kisses
are some of the best things you could ever ask for.
Because even when the person's mind is impaired,
when they can't seem to think clearly,
their mind still knows you're important.
That you're worth putting a little extra effort into.
Like you're engrained into their thoughts
and no amount of alcohol can tear you from their
mind.
So I am thankful for our little drunken paradise.

I cannot keep doing this with you.
You beat me down,
shatter me to pieces.
But somehow I still convince myself
that I'm better when I'm with you.
Yet my mind,
its screaming for me to let you go.
It's not healthy what we do.
I tell myself I hate you only because it's easier
than admitting after everything you've done to me.
You're still the only person on my mind.
Everything is screaming for me to let you go,
yet my heart wants to hold on,
just a little longer.

If two people are meant to be together, they will find their way back to each other. No matter the obstacles in their way. No matter the time, the distance, or the people that try to stand in their way. Don't stress over it, don't worry about it, if it's meant to be then baby one day it will be.

Chasing you was like chasing the sunset,
ever so beautiful until you realized there was never
any chance of catching it.
Yet that didn't stop me from waking up every morning
and trying all over again.

I could drink my body weight in vodka and surround myself with the prettiest of girls, but not even that could wash the taste of you out of my mouth, and not one of them could compare to what I saw in you.

And now I just want to go back to sleep because life is a nightmare and *she's a dream.*

I have everything I've ever thought I'd want. I find myself smiling again, I think I'm happy. Yet every time the clock strikes 11:11 I still find myself wishing she was you.

So there's this girl, and when I see her face I can't even fathom the hours of work God must have put into her. Sculpting her button nose, her big brown eyes, lips so perfectly shaped and pink. And so there's this girl, the way she talks, god yes she may be young but she's wise beyond her years, sentences wrapping around my mind like a perfectly worded novel.

When my eyes are closed
you're the only sight I see.
When my nose is stuffy on a cold winters day
it's like I can still remember how you smelled when
you held me against you.
When I brush my hair
it's like your fingers are still dancing through it.
When I'm taking shots of your favorite liquor
I'd much rather chase it with a kiss from your lips.
When I'm lying in bed at night
and the world is silent,
I can still hear the beating of your heart
as if my head was still on your chest.
And even when you are nowhere to be found
you are everywhere.

And I think you've just gotta find that one person that makes you feel alive. But not only that, you've got to find someone who makes you feel like you're living. Because shit I've been alive for a while, but I've only just started living.

Touch me, in the most intimate of ways. I don't even mean physically, I mean alter my mind, make me think differently because I've met you. Change my point of views, challenge me, touch my life in a way that I'll never be able to forget you. That I'll never be able to walk down the street without something reminding me of you. That when I lie awake at two in the morning it'll be because of something you said. Touch my life, touch my soul, and my mind. Don't just exist in my life, make sure that I'm changed because I met you.

You know when a house becomes a home. You know which stairs creek just a little more than others, you know every turn like the back of your hand and you could walk around in the dark. Well I've had a house but never a home. Until now. Home is the two freckles on your right ear, home is the way you smile just a little crooked, or how the green in your eyes sparkles just a little brighter than the sun. I know what home feels like now, *home feels like you.*

Love. Love isn't having butterflies all the time. I think love is calm. Love is comfortable. I could sit in silence with you for the rest of our lives and it would mean more than a thousand words with anyone else.

I've done a lot of things wrong in my life,
and you know how they say two wrongs don't make a right?
I don’t think that’s true, because all my wrongs have lead me to you,
and baby you sure are right.

I'm afraid of you leaving because I will spend the rest of my days searching for you in everyone I meet.

You're the one I want to tell my kids about 15 years from now when they ask me what love is. I wanna tell them about my first real love, point across the dining room table, and tell them it's their mom. I want them to know they can find the love of their life at 18 the way we did. I wanna tell them about how we met, the things we overcame, the adventures we took, and how I fell in love with the most beautiful girl in the world. You're the one I'll tell my kids about years from now. And if I can't point across the table and tell them it's you, don't worry. I'll still tell them about you. I'll tell everyone.

Inside the cover of my favorite book.

I'm sitting in the same coffee house I met you in for the first time. I have nothing else to write on. But I'm watching these two, coffee in hand. They look and talk as though they are on a first date. I hear her telling him how she got the scar on her hand and what her favorite kind of pizza is (its pepperoni). I can't help but wonder if anyone thought of us here. Did they listen to me tell you about my favorite coffee, how I broke my leg, or how beautiful I thought you were? Did they listen to us laugh, see us smile? I wonder if they thought back to a first date they had in this very coffee shop. I wonder how many first dates this coffee shop has seen, how many relationships it has unknowingly helped to create. How many laughs it has heard, and how much happiness it has created. It sure created some for me. I can only hope I'll be sitting in this coffee shop smiling with you again soon.

Things are changing, but this time I'm not scared.
You came in and changed everything, and I never
wanted it to be the same again.
Change is good. Good with you.

Her. The feeling I get when she's around. The way my heart beats just a little faster and my hands get clammy. But more than that, the way she makes me laugh, and not just giggle, I mean the laugh that comes from the soul and bellows throughout your whole body. The way my heart beats faster but my mind calms down, if even just for a moment. How I could listen to her talk for hours about anything and everything or sit in complete silence but feel just as content either way. The feeling. The feeling you get when you just know. Know you want to be around that person, that you want to make them happy no matter the cost to yourself. The feeling. It's, well, indescribable. It's just. There. She's just, there. But I want her *here.*

I've moved homes 5 times in 4 years. And I've never really stayed anywhere long enough to really let myself develop roots or attachments. Nowhere really felt like home. A house was just a roof over my head and a bed was just somewhere to sleep. Nothing was ever mine. Nothing had meaning. Nothing felt like home. Until you.

My soul has been waiting an eternity for you.

Sometimes there is so much to be said without saying anything at all. There are so many ways to say I love you without uttering those three little words. It's the little things. You know me like the back of your hand. I can tilt my cheek towards you ever so slightly and within moments your lips collide with it. You feel my excitement with the speed in my step and so you walk just a little quicker too. My hand brushes yours and so our fingers intertwine. Sometimes you know me better than I know myself, and I think it means something when someone learns the little things about you without you saying anything at all. You have created a blueprint to my heart without any direction at all. Your love is worth a thousand words. But the difference is it doesn't need any at all.

I was never a morning person until I woke up next to you.
-4:16 am

She likes her coffee light and sweet, mine black and hot, some things so different but I've never fit with anyone better.

I'm looking at your sleepy eyes. Too bad there's a screen and so many miles between us. But for once I feel okay. I feel at ease. My eyes feel heavier and my heart feels lighter. And I wish you knew the things I'd do to wake up next to those sleepy eyes tomorrow.

You have 16 freckles on your back. I counted them as my hands danced on your skin. I thought to myself, if I drew lines connecting them the path might lead straight to my heart.

All I could think of was all the different ways you had touched me. The ways your hands caressed my cheek before you leaned in to kiss me gently. The way they tangled in my hair when you kissed the air out of lungs. The way your fingers interlaced with mine dragging me through the grocery store. Always pulling me along. The hands that washed my hair every day. The ones that picked me up when I was down and held me ever so tightly at night. I look at myself and all I can see is all the ways you've touched me.

I think of you in words that don't even exist.

"Everyone wants to fall in love
But no one expects to fall out of it
And normally
The two go hand in hand,
Just as we used to."

please don't make me fall for you.

"You're stuck with me"
But is it really stuck if I'm exactly where I wanna be?

You said I love you for the first time, as I sat perched on the stairs watching you walk out the door for a weekend business trip. Those three little words left your mouth with such ease, as though you'd been uttering them to me for the last twenty years. Butterflies flew ramped in my stomach, my heart beat out of my chest, yet my mind calmed down. Because I realized you uttered those words to me as though you'd been saying them for twenty years, and in that moment I realized I wanted to listen to you say them for twenty more.

To the ones struggling to go on

Hope
Hope is when he walks into your room and you pretend you're sleeping
Hope is when you hide under your bed
Hope is when you run as fast as your legs can take you
Hope is breaking a plate and thinking he won't notice
Hope is when you think it's the last time
Hope is when you say it will never happen again
but what do you do when all your hope is *gone?*

When I was little they took me to a museum and told me to fall in love with art.
But I didn't see anything worth loving in this world, so I tried to make art out of myself.
Now here I sit covered in scars wondering what's so lovely about this?

I wish that I could explain the feeling that comes with having a mental illness. The complete inability to control your thoughts, emotions, and even actions sometimes. I wish I could accurately put into words what it feels like to feel like a stranger to yourself. The pure amount of effort it takes me to get out of bed some mornings. I wish I could tell someone how mutilated my skin is most days. How bruised my knuckles are, or how heavy my heart is. I wish I could tell you how alone I feel. How much I am hurting. But at the same time I feel nothing. It makes no sense to me. So how could it possibly make sense to anyone else? It feels like my mind is attacking itself. I keep smiling. And I keep saying I'm fine, because I can't even think about where I would start to try to explain to someone how not okay I really am. Mental illness is ruining my life, and those are the only words I can find to try to explain it.

A year ago today you pulled me off the top of a parking garage outside MSU. I told you to just go. To just leave me, but you didn't. You didn't leave, you sat on the top of that parking garage with me as I broke down and I told you how I wanted to die. How I couldn't do it anymore. You didn't understand that it had nothing to do with you. You did everything you could. But the point is, you stayed. You stayed until you convinced me I had just one more day in me, just as you had the day before. I owe you a lot. You loved me even when I didn't love myself. You loved me enough for the both of us. You pulled me off the top of that parking garage and for that I will forever be indebted to you. I'm not here to rehash old relationships or past loves. But today on a road trip home the sun was setting and I got off at the nearest exit. I walked around the harbor and I ran up the stairs in the parking garage overlooking the city, I jumped the ledge and sat with my feet dangling. A man ran over to me, asking if I was alright. I turned around and smiled at him assuring him I was. He sat there with me for a minute just to make sure. I sat with my feet dangling over the edge, took a deep breath and I realized that in that moment I was okay. Don't get me wrong, I'm not always. But when he ran over to me and asked me if I was alright, I realized something. I really didn't want to jump. I sat there until the sun went down and I thought about the last year. And I realized that for the last year I've been alone, and when the sun went down today, I took myself off the edge because now I love myself enough for us both.

Living with a mental illness in your 20's

Hi, my name is Jess and I have a mental illness. This is how I feel I have to introduce myself to people at this point in my life. I'm 20 years old, living with major depressive disorder, PTSD, and an anxiety disorder. I go to therapy, I take medication, but I can get sad, really, really sad sometimes, and I can get angry, really, really angry sometimes. Sometimes I'm not even me. Sometimes I can't get out of bed in the morning, I can't brush my teeth, my hair, go to class, or practice. One minute I'm laughing and the next I'm crying. But I am fighting. Sometimes I am happy, unconditionally so, stable, loving, and healthy. I'll go to class, I'll score the game winning goal, and I'll end up with a 4.0 GPA for the semester. Sometimes you can't even tell I'm living with this dark cloud inside of me. I cannot guarantee you that I will always wake up with a smile on my face, but I promise you this, I love unconditionally, hard, and whole heartedly. I give my all in everything that I do. I work hard. I have more determination inside of me than most people I've met. I've been to hell and back in my almost 21 years, but I've made it back every time. No matter how sad I get, no matter how shitty I get, I will come back from it, I always do, and I always will. So try not to give up on me, because one day I'll be back, *I'll be me again.*

I have been alive for 360 days after trying to take my own life. I sit here in this airport a year later, passport in hand, with a full backpack, but an even fuller heart. And in 3 hours I will be on a plane to a country I've never been to. Today I've taken 2 trains, 6 subways, and countless steps in the right direction. Don't get me wrong, I've tripped and fallen in the last year, but I have gotten up every time. The world has continued to throw punches at me and a few of them stung but nonetheless they healed in time and I got right back in the ring. I have been given every reason to give up, but I am here, I am standing, and I am breathing. *I AM HERE* and that is worth something. So here's to being resilient, here's to being a fighter, and here's to a year of crazy, a year of having my medication changed so many times I lost count, to countless therapy sessions, late night drives, tears, bruises, to the days I couldn't get out bed, shower, or even go to class. But here's to scoring the game winning goal, hitting a new PR in the gym, and laughing till I cried. Here's to jumping out of bed today, here's to being alive after being given every reason not to be. And here's to the ticket I'll be holding a year from now, to somewhere new, because I will be here. *I will be alive.*

Don't let yourself give up. You have survived every one of your bad days. You are still here and that that is worth something. You woke up every day even when you didn't want to. Even when you didn't think you could. You put your feet on the floor and you existed for just one more day. And even if you didn't have the energy to put your feet on the floor that day, you still conquered one more day. Even if you didn't make it out of bed, brush your teeth, or your hair. You did it. You survived just one more day, and that's what you have to keep doing. Because you are resilient, you are a fighter, you are a survivor. Mental illness will not claim you too, because you are so much stronger than you even realize. One day you're going to wake up and you're going jump out of bed to the pitter patter of little feet running down the hall screaming “mommies wake up”. You'll get out of bed, you'll go about your day, and you won't be surviving anymore*, you'll be living.* So keep going, even when it feels like you can't, especially when it feels like you can’t, because one day to going to be okay.

Things will get better, even if it doesn't seem like it right now. The world can be so cruel sometimes, but don't let that make you hard. Don't let it make you numb, don't let it take the love out of your heart. You won't be sad forever. So stay here, stay alive, because amazing things are coming. If you can't get out of bed today that's okay. But make sure you do tomorrow. Listen to your heart but also to your head. Know what you deserve and go after it. Don't give up on the world or yourself, because you have no idea what you're going to accomplish. But you've gotta be alive to see it. Don't let mental illness win this one, no matter how hard it gets, because it will get better, *I promise.*

Homesick for a place that doesn't exist.
A house is not always a home.

The stigma between being mentally ill and taking medication really bothers me. I am not crazy, taking medication does not make me weak, it does not mean I am any less of a person than someone who does not rely on medication. What many don't seem to grasp is that all this medication provides for someone like myself is the missing chemicals, it allows my brain to function as normally as anyone else's would. it's not giving me something extra, it's just providing what others naturally produce. Something I don't. There is nothing wrong with taking medication. It does not make you less of a person. It does not make you weak. It makes you human. For the first time in nearly a year I feel like myself again. For the first time in a year it doesn't feel like there is an elephant sitting on my chest. For the first time in a year I can breathe, I can smile, I can sing in the car. For the first time in nearly a year I have accepted that I am human, and that having the ability to ask for help does not make me weak, only strong. For the first time in nearly a year, I can breathe. For the first time in nearly a year I am me again.

Stay alive no matter how hard it is. No matter how harsh the world can get or how cold and unaccepting people may be. Stay alive no matter how sad, angry, or hopeless you may feel. Because they are just that, feelings, and feelings fade and change. Stay alive no matter what happens because there is nothing more important. Anything. ANYTHING can be changed or manipulated over time to be something else. Anything but death. Because death doesn't change. It just is. That is one decision that no letter, no text, no "I'm sorry" can fix. It is permanent and everything else is temporary. Sometimes things get so hard and the world gets so dark. But that will change. It will fade. But the light you leave with others won't, the happiness you bring, the laughs you create, those things go on forever. So no matter what happens, no matter how sad, dark, or unbearable things get

Stay alive.

June 4th, 2016/VI-IV-MMXVI

Think about the hardest day of your life. This was mine. It's the day I tried to take my own life, it's the day I finally accepted help and all that would bring for me. I admitted to having a mental illness and to the fact that I could no longer fight that battle on my own. I spent so many years suffering in silence, afraid to openly talk about this struggle, because society told me I was crazy. I wish more than anything that when I was younger someone would have talked this openly about mental illness, because maybe then 19-year-old me wouldn't have felt so alone. *No one should want to take their own life before it has even really begun.* Some may think it's stupid to have such a date tattooed on me for the rest of my life, but that in itself is why I got this. My life could have ceased to exist on that very day, and so every day since then has been a victory. It has been one hell of a year and a half for me. I've had my medication changed so many times I've lost count, I've spent countless hours in therapy, I've changed therapists, psychologists. I've felt low, I've felt high, and I've landed somewhere between the two, a place I like to call *okay*. I don't feel so alone anymore; I recognize the love around me. Even on my worst days, I recognize that everything won't always be okay, and I'm going to get sad again, but I'm going to get through it. It's a bad day, not a bad life. I've grown immensely and become a person I am proud of. I've experienced so much in only the last year and a half and to think that I could have missed out on all that laughter, those smiles, experiences, and people, is insane to me. I'm thankful for this day, because without it, I wouldn't be who I am today. This isn't the end for me, and it isn't for you either. For anyone who's struggling let me tell you to keep going. You have no idea how much good there is in the world, how much love you have to give and receive. Please don't give up, and don't be afraid to ask for help. You are so much more than your mental illness. But most importantly, it will get better, so take it from me. ***Stay alive. It's worth it.***

To those of you that made it this far, thank you. Let this book remind you that no matter what you've been through and no matter what your going through, that even through the darkest parts,

You have bloomed.